SIXTY YEARS

Selected Poems

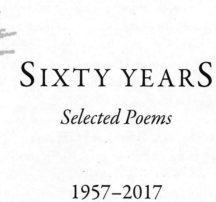

Mikhail Yeryomin

Михаил Ерёмин

Sixty yearS

Selected Poems

1957–2017

translated by J. Kates

BLACK
WIDOW
PRESS

Boston

Black Widow Press is an imprint of Commonwealth
Books, Inc., Boston, MA. Distributed to the trade by NBN
(National Book Network) throughout North America, Can-
ada, and the U.K. All Black Widow Press books are printed on
acid-free paper, and glued into bindings. Black Widow Press
and its logo are registered trademarks of Commonwealth
Books, Inc.

Joseph S. Phillips and Susan J. Wood, Ph.D., Publishers
www.blackwidowpress.com

Design & production: Kerrie L. Kemperman
Plant illustration (cover and pages 2–3) by Olga K. Pastuchiv,
used with permission of the artist.

ISBN-13: 978-1-7371603-1-1

Printed in the United States
10 9 8 7 6 5 4 3 2 1

Some of the translations in this collection have been previously published in *Contrappasso, Exchanges, The Fjords Review, Hawai'i Review, Naked Punch, North Dakota Quarterly, Parthenon West, Pusteblume, Stand, Two Lines, World Literature Today,* and in the anthology *In the Grip of Strange Thoughts* (Zephyr: 1999) as well as in *Selected Poems 1957–2009* (White Pine: 2014).

Михаил ЕРЁМИН

СтихотворениЯ

Кн. 7

ПУШКИНСКИЙ ФОНД
САНКТ-ПЕТЕРБУРГ • MMXVII

TRANSLATOR'S INTRODUCTION

When I sought a cover image for this expanded selection of Mikhail Yeryomin's poems, I looked first to Harvard University's collection of glass flowers crafted by the Blaschka family in the nineteenth century. These consummate works of art and science might, above all else, be emblematic of what goes on in so many of Yeryomin's poems, a creative tension and symbiosis between organic growth and artificial reproduction, a microscopically crystalline eye focused on the effusion of nature. The museum refused me permission to reproduce an image unless "the poetry was about or inspired by the collection." Their loss. In the world, there are correspondences not discernible as direct links or causal relationships — leaps from one discipline to another, and Yeryomin's poetry makes these leaps on every page. If ever there was a poet who has followed Blake's injunction to see infinity in a grain of sand and heaven in a wildflower, that poet is Mikhail Yeryomin. For his own books in the original, the poet has used no cover image at all, simply the designation "Poems" and a book number.

For more than half a century, Yeryomin[1] has been writing these poems unique in Russian literature. Each of more than two hundred fifty poems (so far) is a discrete eight-line stanza. When he publishes them, each one takes up a separate page. Some are accompanied by notes. After six decades now, these form a sweep of verse that has its only English analogue, perhaps, in Berryman's *Dream Songs* or Pound's *Cantos,* and none at all in Russian poetry. (In a French tradition, Maurice Scève's Renaissance sequence *Délie: Objet de plus haute vertu* may come closest to Yeryomin's

---

[1]   In an academic transliteration of the poet's name, it is written *Eremin.* The poet himself prefers a transliteration that more closely approximates the English pronunciation. Because he has been published in German translation also (*V.* the anthology *Moderne russische Poesie seit 1966,* ed. Walter Thümler, Oberbaum Verlag, Berlin: 1990) his surname sometimes appears as *Jerjomin.* Another translator, Alex Cigale, has published some of his own English translations using the transliteration "Eremin."

achievement, but the virtuous love-object of the Russian poet's obsession is the whole living world over a stretch of time from Creation until now.)

Mikhail Fyodorovich Yeryomin was born in 1936 in the northern Caucasus but grew up in Leningrad, where he studied in the Philology Department of the Leningrad State University and graduated from the Herzen Institute. A close friend and associate of Joseph Brodsky before that poet's exile, Yeryomin is a playwright and a translator (of T.S. Eliot[2], Hart Crane, W.B. Yeats, M. Ikbal, Khushkhal-khan Khattak, among others) who saw few of his poems published in his homeland during the Soviet period. Instead, his work appeared in émigré journals like *Kontinent* and *Ekho*. The first volume of his poems (in Russian) was published in the United States in 1986, and then in 1991 in Moscow. In 2013, the first manuscript of my translations of Yeryomin into English won the Cliff Becker Book Prize in Translation. That included the poet's writing only through 2004, but the book as finally published by White Pine Press in 2014 added poems through 2009. Nearly every book of his is a cumulative edition to and a selection from his previous work, and each carries the same title: *СтихотворениЯ* (PoemS)[3]. The most recent comprehensive collection, published in Moscow in 2021, incorporates a number of revisions of earlier poems. *Sixty Years* reflects those revisions both in the original Russian and in my translations[4]. It is more than half again as large as the earlier *Selected Poems*.

Among other distinctions, Yeryomin was awarded the Andrey Bely Prize in 1999 and honored with a Brodsky Fellowship in 2014.

---

[2] Yeryomin's choice of Eliot's "Usk" and "Rannoch, by Glencoe" from "Landscapes," printed in *СтихотворениЯ, кн.* 6, 2016, shows a close affinity with his own work.

[3] With one exception, a 2018 selection called *Его, Ему, Им и о Нём*.

[4] The most telling of these revisions is the replacement of an abstract noun *соблазн*, temptation, with the concrete *яблоко*, apple.

The best description of Yeryomin's poetry comes from Mikhail Aizenberg's comprehensive essay "A Few Others"[5]:

"Generally speaking, there is no school you could put Eremin [Yeryomin] in, even conditionally.... The assigned eight-line canon, the absence (except for his early verse) of rhyme — all this is no accident. In general, Eremin's texts can contain nothing accidental. the verse's superdense fabric would offer terrible resistance to anything too free or casual.... [T]he verbal transformations obey their own laws, and the poems grow like crystals.... They strive to take in everything, to become everything.... This kind of poetics, woven together with maximally intense thought, has no direct analogues or traces of obvious influences."

Nevertheless, Yeryomin has been associated with the Leningrad "Philological School" of the 1960s and 70s embracing primarily Vladimir Uflyand, Leonid Vinogradov, Sergey Kulle, Mikhail Krasilnikov, Yuri Mikhailov, Aleksandr Kondratov, and Lev Losev as well as Yeryomin, which was experimenting with the possibilities of *vers libre* when that kind of thing was generally treated warily in Russian poetry. It flourished as a community until the emigration of Losev in the mid 1970s. Yeryomin's work stands out even from the work of his close contemporaries and associates by the abundant variety embedded in his steadfast regularity of form.

"In the original Russian," Ilya Kaminsky has written, "Yeryomin, who was one of the first (and very few) poets in his generation to drop rhyme, was able to find a new kind of music that was multi-vocal, and surprising. At the core, there is something very metaphysical, very transformative about Yeryomin's work.... There is something other-worldly about these poems, how they use the vocabulary of cannons, ship-building, cows, breakfast eggs, soccer fields, and yet they enter into a 'sky of rooms.' In these lines, animals put on 'shoes in snowy tracks' into an earth that

---

[5] Translated by Marian Schwartz in *Russian Studies in Literature,* spring 1996, pp 28–9.

wishes 'both for darkness and light.' In the contemporary Russian literary community, Yeryomin is — without a doubt — a metaphysician for our times."

Working with these poems can call on an encyclopedic knowledge, or compel me to compile one. Physical dictionaries heap up on my desk until I look and feel like a medieval portrait of Saint Jerome, while on-line resources reproduce on an electronic screen. Some poems ask me to call on my memory of Osip Mandelstam's poetry and send me re-reading four chapters of the Book of Revelation; others return me to a body of Pushkin's work that is immediately accessible to every literate Russian but not to a foreign reader unsteeped in the literature. While natural and scientific references are readily accessible to a translator and a general reader, cultural allusions prove wonderfully rich and particularly vexing. If I were to translate each one of these references literally, I would lose the reader in a distracting wilderness; if I were to footnote them all, I would sink the poems in scholarly quicksand. Best to let the reader know they are there, create equivalents where possible, and let the rest go, as an encouragement for readers to learn the originals inside and out. The only notes here are Yeryomin's own, in the original texts.

I can spend days worrying just a line or two, like the proverbial dog with its favorite bone. I leave it and walk around, read or solve a crossword puzzle, split wood or clean house, coming back again and again to this word and that one, changing vocabulary and syntax for rhythm, rhythm for assonance. Slowly these sets of eight lines fill out, fill in. Throughout, I have been guided and warned by William Butler Yeats in "Adam's Curse": "A line will take us hours maybe; / Yet if it does not seem a moment's thought, / Our stitching and unstitching has been naught."

Because Yeryomin has his own command of English, I can work more closely with him than with many of the other poets I translate. I have been grateful not only to the poet for his own patient explanations, but also for the occasional assistance of others, especially as I probed mysteries of Slavonic vocabulary and allusion. From Michael Molnar I took one noun early on, as it was a better choice than another I had settled on. Grigory Benevich, Charles Koch, Dmitry Manin, and Aleksandr Porvin, among the names I can remember, have all provided specific, invaluable help. Dennis Maloney guided the earlier White Pine selection to publication, and Joe Phillips and Kerrie Kemperman have made this book possible. To these, and to others unnamed, I acknowledge a dependency. Language is a common on which we all graze our flocks, intermingling, drawing sustenance, and manuring it again out of our own stocks.

As a translator, I am more opportunistic than theoretical. My aim has been to convey in English, by whatever means necessary, the content and force of the original, and I am flexible in my approach — sometimes adhering closely to original formal constructs, sometimes deviating from them. Yeryomin's work demands the eight-line format, sensitivity to technical terms, rhythms and word-play. Rhythms, of course, are as much linguistic constructs as words and idioms. In at least one case, Yeryomin invited me to translate what lies behind the words, rather than what the words themselves indicate. In another case, he asked for a rhythmic impossibility in English. Equivalence therefore sometimes replaces congruence.

Yeryomin has been publishing his poems for more than sixty years now, and I have been translating some of them for half that time. During these decades, we have been in each other's company in person hardly at all — probably less than a week if we total up all the brief meetings; the poems themselves have constituted our community. Even as I write these notes, I have been sent a new compilation of Yeryomin's poetry encompassing his entire *œuvre*, moving into 2019 and 2020.

Im Norden auf Kahler Höh

....

Er traeumt von finer Palme
Heinrich Heine[6]

Plants have memory (Hypothesis)

It may be, during its cold winter sleep, a tree
Scrolls through its annual rings,
Some pleasant, some harsh,
Passes over the vague recollection
Of origin (the fusion of gametes)
And plunges deep (through the memory of its karyotype)

Into time immemorial to a marvelous garden
With charming woodland creatures.

2018

In a recent e-mail note to me about one of the last poems in this collection, Yeryomin wrote, "a tall old tree never has rest, even when everything goes quiet, its own branches crackle, like old joints. Yours ME"

And now, reader, yours.

---

[6] *In the north on a barren height /... / It dreams about a palmtree* (tr. A. Z. Foreman)

Боковитые зёрна премудрости,
Изначальную форму пространства,
Всероссийскую святость и смутность
И болот журавлиную пряность
Отыскивать в осенней рукописи,
Где следы оставила слякоть,
Где листы, словно платья луковицы,
Слезы прячут в складках.

1957

Polyhedral kernels of wisdom,
Primordial form of space.
All-Russian holiness, hodgepodge
And the herony tang of swampland
To be searched out in autumnal writing,
Where the slush has left its traces,
Where leaves, like the skirts of an onion
Conceal tears in their creases.

1957

Сшивает портниха на швейной машинке,
Подобно дождю, голубое с зеленым,
Дождю, который окном изломан,
Как лодкою камышинки.
Гром за окном покашливает.
Капли дождя к стеклу прилипают,
Полузеленая каждая
И полуголубая.

1957

The seamstress stitches on a sewing machine,
Light blue with deep green, like rain,
Rain broken by the window
As reeds are broken by a little boat.
A thunderstorm coughs outside the window.
Raindrops cling to the glass,
Every single one of them half green
And half light blue.

1957

Л. Лифшицу

Переплавил не в золото — в никель
Рыжий алхимик снега.
На небе, как в Голубиной книге,
Еврейская грамота березняка.
Равнины черны, как раввины,
Заполнены реки щепой от весла,
В совиных глазнцах овинов,
Как мышь, зашуршала весна.

1957

for L. Lifshitz

The auburn alchemist of snow
Transmuted not into gold but nickel.
In the heavens, as in the Book of Doves,
A Hebrew primer of birches.
Ravines as black as rabbis,
Rivers running with shards of oars,
In owlish eye-sockets of granaries,
Spring, like a mouse, was rustling.

1957

Пальба из-под ног уходила, как палуба,
Падал пушкарь на осеннюю подстилку,
Словно батальонный баловень
Бил о поле затылком.
Павшего запеленает в кисет,
Формалином и соком древесным пропахший,
Маркитант-носитель косы
памяти императора Павла.

1958

A cannonade careered underfoot like an anchor-deck,
The gunner downed on the autumn detritus,
As the pet of a battalion
Bumped the back of his head on the boards.
The pig-tailed sutler swaddles the fallen one
in a tobacco-pouch,
permeated with formaline and sap,
a pavilion commemorating the Emperor Paul.

                                        1958

Там тени павших пашут ресницах,
Там, в царстве доадамовой смекалки,
Кентавры негодуют по-оленьи,
В соперников втыкая томагавки.

1958

Там, кумачом завесив небо комнат,
Перистый вепрь выпрыгивает в дым;
Нагие ноги ноют в катакомбах,
Перебираемые, как лады.

1958

There shadows plough fallen eyelashes,
There, in the realm of pre-adamic intelligence,
Centaurs take umbrage like deer,
Burying tomahawks into competitors.

1958

There, a sky of rooms hung with red calico,
A feathery wild boar breaks out into the smoke;
Naked legs lament in the catacombs,
Being fingered like harmonies.

1958

Строил первого в мире моста
К месту строительства бревна таскал и доски,
Ладил настил, а потом настал
Час первой повозки.
Плотник локти положил на перила,
Трубкой украсил довольное лицо,
Выплеснул на рубаху бороды белила,
И стало мостостроение ремеслом отцов.

1958

The builder of the first bridge in the world
Dragged beams and boards to the construction site,
Readied the planking — and then began
The hour of the first vehicle.
The carpenter laid his elbows on the railing,
His contented face adorned by a pipe,
Whitewash splashed on the bib of his beard,
And bridgebuilding became an ancestral craft.

1958

Тёрлось тельце телка
Об устойчивые стены стойла.
Нос коровий тельца толкал
Выводил на пустырь просторный.
Теленок вышел из коровника,
Стадности не стыдясь, пересёк пустырь
И нежился в поле перстым курортником,
Жил, пережевывая стебли и лепестки.

1958

The cow cuddled the calf
All through the stalls of the stable,
The cow's nose nudged the calf
Out into the open lot.
The calf came out of the cow-barn
Ahead of the herd, loped through the lot
And basked in the field like a dappled sunbather,
Asked for nothing but stems and petals.

                                        1958

По-за кряквой ходит селезень,
То прищёлкнет клювом плоским,
То крылом взмахнет, как сеятель,
Глазом ласковым поблескивая,
Чтоб, живущий возле заводи,
Мальчуган нашел гнездо,
Чтоб яи́шенные завтраки
Подавала мать на стол.

1958

The drake pays court to the duck,
He snaps his flat beak,
He swings his wing like a man sowing seed,
His affectionate eye glitters now and again,
So that the good boy who lives
Near the creek can find the nest,
So his mother can serve up eggs
At the breakfast table.

1958

Сохатый крест рогов, как идола,
Возно́сит над кустарником.
Корову не выигрывает, а выпиливает
Из самых нежных мышц соперника.
Звучит в юдо́ли гонный рог
И ранит бок до соли.
Вдыхают ва́женки пригожие
Жестокий запах отца и сына.

1959

An elk lifts a cross of branching antlers,
like an idol, over the underbrush.
He cuts out his right to the cow
From the tenderest muscles of his rival.
The implacable antler clacks in the glen
And inflicts a wound deep in the flank,
While comely virgin doe breathe in
The cruel scent of father and son.

1959

Золотое перышко выпало из облака,
Словно колечко из наволочки.
Бабушкины сумерки в окна заболоченные
Барабанят острыми ягодами волчьими.
Над крыльцом опята эоловой цепочкой.
Ноги светлым мячиком по ступенькам спрыгивают,
Каждая туфелька подобна красной шапочке,
Лукошку с белыми подарками.

                                                        1960

A golden little plume fell out of a cloud,
Like a ringlet of down from a pillow.
Grandmother's twilight drums with pointed
Wolfish berries on the swampy windows.
Over the porch æolian mushrooms in single file.
Feet hop down the steps like a bright little ball,
Each shoelet like a little red riding hood,
A handbasket filled with white gifts.

1960

Печальный сезон многобожья,
Изломанность зонтичных над падшей травой,
Языческий плач чернобелых болот,
Из прозрачных деревьев сотворение терема,
Утренней церкви заоконное пение,
Стакан золотого заморского чая,
Свеча, обнаженная светом небесным,
И юная дева в преддверье плеча.

1961

A sorrowful season of polytheism,
Fractured umbellifrates over fallen grass,
A pagan lament of blackandwhite marshland,
The creation of a tower from transparent trees,
Plainchant through the windows of morning churches,
A glass of golden tea from abroad,
A candle undressed by a heavenly light,
And a young virgin on the threshold of a shoulder.

1961

Животные обуваются в снежные следы
Или впадают в логово.
Растения гонимы холодом
В лабиринты корней и луковиц.
Люди уменьшают до размеров обуви
Присущие водоемам ладьи.
Подо льдом, как под теплым небом,
Фотолуг, Фотолес, Фотолето.

1962

Animals put on their shoes in snowy tracks
Or go to ground.
Plants tormented by the cold
Into labyrinths of roots and bulbs.
People shrink as small as shoes
Like little boats on reservoirs.
Under the ice, as under a warm sky,
Photomeadow, photowood, photosummer.

                                          1962

$$k = 0$$

И дробь це больших прожекторов
Стоящих валит с ног на тень.
Подобный обескнииженной этажерке
Парит би-Планк над Т Ньютона,
Над часовыми, значительными, как пожарные,
Над живородящими тополями,
Над белковым покровом России,
Библиотекой и футбольным полем.

1963

$$k = 0$$

And the slash of the large searchlights
Fells what's standing into shadow.
The same way, on a bookcase drained of books,
B-Planck swoops over T Newton,
Over watchmen as meaningful as firefighters,
Over viviparous poplars,
Over the albuminous shroud of Russia,
A library and a soccer field.

1963

$a^3 + y^3 - 3axy$ есть ничто.
Ствол не насос, а высохший колодец.
Изоамиламина генератор
Жует подземные лучи.
Нелетний свет слепит растения.
Кольчуга склеренхимы холодна.
Засвечены фотоладони клёнов.
Горит осины санбенито.

1966–8

[Их куб плюс игрек куб минус три а икс игрек...] — «Декартов лист»

Изоамиламин — пахучее вещество, выделяемое самкой майского жука

$a^3 + y^3 - 3axy$ is nothingness.
A tree-trunk is not a pump, but a dry well.
A generator of isoamilamin
Munches on underground rays.
An unsummery light dazzles the plants.
Cold is the mail-shirt of sklerenchemistry.
The photopalms of maples overexposed.
The sanbenito of the aspen flames.

                    1966–8

x cube plus y cube minus three axy: the "Folium of Descartes" = jasmine leaf

isoamilamin is a strong-smelling substance given off by the female may-bug

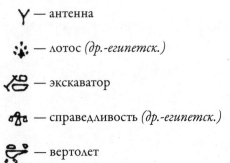

Гелиопте́р гостиницы высотной,
Как перистое небо над поблекшим
Пришкольным сквером.
Владелицы осенних ранцев
Трепещут над сетями «классов»,
Уносит вдаль летучки кленов
Поток асфальта, огибая сквер.

1971

Y — антенна

— лотос *(др.-египетск.)*

— экскаватор

— справедливость *(др.-египетск.)*

— вертолет

Helioptér of a skyscraper hotel,
Like a feathery sky over a faded
Public park beside a school.
The owners of autumnal knapsacks
Tremble over networks of hopscotch.
A flow of asphalt circling the park
Carries the maple wings far away.

1971

Y — antenna

— lotus (ancient Egyptian)

— backhoe

— justice (ancient Egyptian)

— helicopter

Зрю кумиры изваянны...
Г. Р. Державин

Подобный медной орхидее
Кентавр о двух стволах
Воздушный корень изогнул,
Чешуйчатый и ядовитый.
Как между префиксом с суффиксом,
Змея меж πέτρος и Петром. Вечнозеленый
(Не хлорофилл, а $CuCO_3$)
Вознесся лавровый привой.

1972

I behold idols carved...
G. R. Derzhavin

Exactly like a coppery orchid,
A centaur with two trunks
Entwined an airy root
Scaly and venomous.
As between prefix and suffix,
A snake between πέτρος and Peter. Evergreen
(Not chlorophyll, but $CuCO_3$)
a graft of laurel reared up.

1972

Над сквером дом — букет вечерних окон.
Собор от мира сквером огражден.
Лист золотой намотан, словно локон,
На ту же ветвь, которой был рожден.
Осенний день, на грех и слезы падкий,
Молчанье и раскаянье поймет,
Оставив пепел от письма в лампадке
И в медальоне дьявола помет.

1972

The house over the park is a bouquet of evening windows.
A cathedral fenced off from the world by a garden.
A golden leaf is wound like a ringlet
On the very twig that gave it birth.
An autumn day, susceptible to sin and tears,
Will understand silence and repentance,
Ashes of a letter have been left in the icon-lamp
And devil's dung in the medallion.

1972

Посёлок (В сумерках туман подобен
Прасубстантиву: наблюдатель — «...пред
Святым Его Евангелием и животворящим
Крестом...» — становится свидетелем аблактировки
Инфинитива и супина.) сходство
С полузатопленным челном и средним членом
Сравненья мышц стрижа с пружиною зажима,
Забытого на бельевой веревке, обретает.

                                        1977

A settlement (In twilight a fog similar
To the protosubstantive: the observer — "before
His Holy Gospel and life-giving
Cross..." becomes a witness of the ablactation
Of the infinitive and the supine.) is a simulacrum
of a kindled canoe and the middling member
of the comparison of a martin's muscles with an elastic clamp,
forgotten on a linen rope, found.

1977

Повилика, прильнувшая к стеблю,
Бледный витень, чье тело длиной с его жизнь —
Дериват ли от vita? Гаплогия
Композиты из vita и тень?
Или плеть? Аксельбант родовитого льна
Или ядопровод? Или тирса лоза? Или —
«... The laws impressed on matter by the Creator... »
Селекционерская гордость Мойр?

1977

Гаплогия — гаплология.

Ch. Darwin, M. A. *The Origin of Species.* "Recapitulation and conclusion."

A dodder clinging tightly to its stem,
Pallid viten, a body long as its life —
Does it derive from *vita*? Haplogy
Compounded from *vita* and *tenebræ*?
Or a lash? An aiguilette of aristocratic flax
Or a poison duct? Or a vine of thyrsus? Or —
"...*the laws impressed on matter by the Creator...*" —
The selectionist pride of the three Fates?

1977

Haplogy = haplology

Ch. Darwin, M. A. *The Origin of Species*. "Recapitulation and conclusion."

Растениям и тьма, и свет желанны.
(Догадка элинна: *νυχθ-ήμερον* — не зло-добро, а сутки.)
В их верованьях нет ни прозорливых звезд,
Ни страха перед полночью, ни крика петуха,
Ни мрака преисподней, ни паденья ниц пред солнцем —
Им представляется Творец утро-вечерний цветом.
Спряжение глагола «быть» — модель
Метагенеза (и бессмертия) былинки.

1977

νυχθ-ήμερον — ночь-день

Plants wish for both darkness and light.
(The Greeks guessed: νυχθ-ήμερον is not evil-good, but the
day's round.)
Their faith includes neither sagacious stars,
Nor any fear of midnight, nor any cock-crow,
Nor gloom of the Underworld, nor groveling sun-worship —
The morning-evening Creator introduces flowering to them.
The conjugation of the verb "to be" is a pattern
Of the metagenesis (and immortality) of a blade of grass.

1977

νυχθ-ήμερον = night-day

Сомкнула веки. Не вступать, а погружаться
В сокрытый ими сад. Деревья —
Еще не алфавит, уже не древние аллеи текста.
Любовь — еще вторая изгородь. Движенье —
Уже не ноша, но еще не ниша.

Не словом открывают губы
Лучистый взгляд жемчужин
Над моим лицом.

1978

She closed her eyelids. Not to step into, but be plunged
Into a garden hidden beneath them. The trees
Not yet alphabet, now no longer ancient alleys of text.
Love is still a second hedge. Movement
No longer burdensome, but even less a burrow.

Lips do not discover with a word
The radiant appearance of pearls
Over my face.

                                              1978

Пир августа. Азы́чество лампасов и лампад.
Ватрушка — в каждом угольке готовый вспыхнуть
Зелёным пламенем творожный язычок —
Подсолнуха. Стручок гороха скалит зубы,
Расколотый, изогнутый древнейшей шуткой
Равновеликости на взгляд с земли
Луны и соднца. Платье юной горожанки —
Поблекший крапп, полегший лен.

1979

Крапп — марена

Feast of August. Aborigin of trouser-stripes and icon-lamps.
Cheesecake — in each corner ready to flare up
A little cottage-cheese tongue like a green flicker —
Sunflowers. A peapod bares its teeth,
Disruptive, twisted like an ancient joke
Equivalence in looking from the earth
Moon and sun. The dress of a young townswoman —
Withering madder, flattened flax.

1979

Отпавший от высокой ветви лист
Немеет, оказавшись на обочине,
Трепещет, как чахоточная грудь,
Переворачивается четыре раза,
Хватая воздух беззащитным телом,
И, распластавшись, замирает, медленней,
Чем ликогалы выполз, превращаясь
В шепот ветхой трубки.

                                        1980

A leaf that fell from the high branch
Goes mute, having landed on the side of the road,
It trembles, like a consumptive breast,
Turns itself over and over four times,
Gulping the air by its defenseless body,
And having sprawled, grows still, more slowly,
Than the crawl of a lycogalla becoming
The whisper of a decrepit pipelet.

                                        1980

И странствовал,
Совсем как тот, чьё бытиé — не чаша ли
Той трещины,
Прозрачный волосок которой
От сотворения в каолинит заложен
Единственным свидетелем того,
Что видится нам в гефсимáнской тишине
Под сводом сада.

1981

And he wandered
Exactly like him whose existence — is it not a chalice
And cracked
Whose transparent hairlet introduced
From the Creation into kaolinite
By the only witness of what
Appears to us in the quiet of Gethsemane
Under the garden arch.

1981

Возня без названия в зарослях
Брусники и призрак —
В чужом непрозрачном плаще — слизняка,
И дряблые логвища водяной мелюзги,
И алчет, в дупле притаясь, фиолетовый
Прыжок, и теряющий векторность вечер
Не волен в трелевочных ковах и бледен,
Словно Нарцисс с ссадиной от скулы до скулы.

1983

There is a nameless bustling in the thicket
Of red whortleberry and a ghost —
In the opaque, and someone else's raincoat — of a slug,
And the flaccid dens of aquatic small fry,
And the violet leap, hiding in a hollow, starves
while the evening, losing its vector,
Is entrapped in its hobbles and pale,
Like Narcissus with a scratch from cheek to cheek.

1983

Валькирии томятся о шахиде.
Поток шоссе вращает подливные
Колеса. Алущий ручей гюрзы
Противу перистальтики бархана
Струится. С талней песочного хронометра оса
Ныряет вглубь своей обители. Течет
Отара вверх по склону. Вещ
Лакунами протектор минарета.

1985

Valkyries languish over a shakhid.
The torrent of the highway turns an undershot
Paddlewheel. The hungering rivulet of a viper
Streams against the peristalsis
Of a sand-dune. A wasp with an hour-glass
Waist dives deep into its dwelling. A flock
Of sheep flows up the slope.
Lacunæ of the minaret's protector enclose a prophecy.

1985

На подступах к развенчанной столице
И царственна,
Как бронзовый каузатив, что оживлен
Лишь мёртвой зеленью, подобной
Подтекам ив, река,
И прописные — киноварь по медной сини — вербы
На противоположном берегу
Безмолвны.

1985

On the approaches to the deposed capital,
Still regal,
Like a bronze causative, which is animated
Only by a dead green, similar
To the dripping of weeping willows, the river,
And uppercase — vermilion on copper blue — willows
On the opposite shore
Speechless.

1985

Следить бег низких облаков
И пресмыкание далекой электрички. Pópulus Vulgaris
Толпой (Избранничество — не искус ли?)
И вдоль дорог выстраивается. Проникнуть
Ленотром или (Оттиск аватары
На глине или благодать?) Алкидом —
Одна двенадцатая дюжины побед —
В усадьбу Гесперид?

1985

Ленотр — Версальский парк, Фонтенбло и т. д.

To follow the races of low clouds
And the reptilian crawl of a distant train. *Pópulus Vulgaris*
En masse (Isn't a referendum a temptation?)
And alongside, the construction of roads. To penetrate
By means of Le Nôtre or (The Impression of an avatar
In clay, or a blessing?) with Alcides —
One twelfth of a dozen victories —
In the Garden of the Hesperides?

1985

Le Nôtre — The park at Versailles, Fontainebleau, etc.

Фонарь. Отсутствие. Аптека.
И ртутна наледь на металле
Патрульного автомобиля. В тарлатановых тюниках
Метель разучивает па сколопендреллы.
А полуптица-полутяжесть
Белее крыльев, явственных во сне.
И ни задатка, и ни предостережения
Не отразили святочные зеркала.

1986

Streetlamp. Something missing. Drugstore.
And an icy crust like mercury on the metal
Of a patrol car. In tarlatan tutus
The snow storm studies the dance-step of scolopendrella.
But semibird and semiburden
Is whiter than wings distinct in a dream.
And Yuletide mirrors reflected
Neither good luck nor a warning.

                                                    1986

Надичествовать как орфографическое «твёрдо»
В несчастный час,
Когда под городом ворочается пустота
И рвутся цепи звонких окон,
Освобождая грани
От крепости углов,
А путник, соболезнуя владельцам штучной ру́хляди,
Иму́ществует без потерь.

1987

To be present like an orthographic "aitch"
In an unhappy hour,
When the void tosses and turns under the city
And chains of ringing windows burst,
Liberating the walls
From the from the firmness of angles,
But a wayfarer, sympathizing with the owners of inherited
    goods,
Takes indifferent possession.

1987

Оставив девочек в декокте мелководья, девой
Явиться из ребра вольны.
Бесследно отмель миновав, на берег
Взойти — разводистые лунки
По ситцу. Грудь и бёдра
(У кончика ноги цветущий подорожник.)
Оправить вязкой сетью.
И множиться в зрачках и на устах.

1987

Girls left in a decoction of shallows, a virgin
Emerges from the edge of a wave.
Without leaving a trace in the sand, to climb up
On the berm — discolored openings
In the chintz. Breast and thigh
(A plantain flowering at the stem of her leg,)
Set right in an intractable net.
Burgeoning deep in the eyes and on the lips.

1987

Нет, не грустить о славных временах
Народных пирожков с начинкой
Из ливера эретико́в, — но, скажем, примерять личины
(Напялил, сдовно маску, кости таза,
Изящно позвоночник изгонул,
Подобно хоботу противогаза,
И стал неузнаваем Вельзеву́л.) и
Беседовать о самоценности плаце́бо.

1992

No, not to grieve for the celebrated times
Of folkloric pies stuffed with
The guts of heretics, — but, let's say, to try on disguises
(I put on, like a mask, pelvic bones,
A spinal column gracefully bent
Like the proboscis of a gas-mask,
And became unrecognizable Beelzebub.) and
To chat about the placebo of self-worth.

                                                    1992

Полночна констелля́ция,
Пруд — лоно лунно — без морщинки,
И — тени, тени, тени... — акустическое одиночество.
Упругую поверхность возмутить
(Затрепетала спугнутая элоде́я.)
Припав губами. Жажда —
Извечнее
И при́снее воды?

1992

Midnight constellation,
A pond — lunar lapping — without a ripple,
And — shadows, shadows, shadows... — acoustical solitude.
To agitate an elastic surface
(Exhausted frightened elodea.)
Lips have pressed. Is thirst
more sempiternal
and more everlasting than water?

                                                    1992

Владеть устами — навык или дар,
Когда молчание билабиальней речи? Окольцовывать
(Orbicularis oris) или отвергать.
А гений, ставший на крыло
(Лазоревые кроющие перья, маховые —
Пребелые.), не зависает ли,
Быв удостоен невесомым «Ах!» меж алых семядолей,
Их разомкунувшим?

1992

Is it skill or a gift to govern the lips
When silence is more bilabial than speech? To band
(Orbicularis oris) or to turn away.
And genius, on the wing
(Sky-blue covering feathers beating
Blindingly white.) hovering, yes?
With an earned, weightless "Ah!" among scarlet cotyledons
It had dispersed?

1992

Ириаде

И ликовать
И вдруг впадать в отчаянье, пока одушевленно
Кипение
Ещё в стога не сложенного луга
И близок профиль спутицы на фоне
Лило́во — ро́зовый намёт, подложенный
Лазурью, — ви́дной
Зари.

1993

for Iraida

And rejoice,
And suddenly fall into despair while a lively
Boiling
Still roils the unstacked hay of an open meadow
Nearby, my beloved's profile — on a violet
Background, a gathering of pink, lined
With azure — visible
Dawn.

1992

Будь суждено — *in contumacia* —
Тогда и с палубным билетом
На бра́ндере в лонгше́зе
Дремать бы или, на худой конец,
Заняться систематизированием антецеде́нтных
Случайностей и совпадений,
Ан нет — ни выволоченного (Кем?)
На брег челна, ни паруса на горизонте.

1995

Be it judged — *in contumacia* —
And then with a deck ticket
On a fireship in a chaise longue
To doze or if worse came to worst
To be busy with the systemization of antecedents
Of accidents and coincidences,
And nothing to be done — neither a boat dragged
    (by Whom?)
Onto shore, nor a sail on the horizon.

                                        1995

Войти под кров древесных крон (Фитоцено́з
На третий день Творения?), как в храм,
Понéже лесом осязаемо движение
И ви́димо кипрéйным гарям
И вейниковым вырубкам,
И не у всякого дыхания,
Но у растений —
Не сказано ли? — пренатальный опыт смерти.

1996

To go in under the forest canopy (Phytocenosis
On the third day of Creation) as into a temple,
For that the movement in the woods is tangible
And visible to the willow cinders
And to the birch clearings,
And not to just any breathing,
But to plant-growth —
Hasn't it been said? — there is a prenatal experience of death.

                                                    1996

Просторной стороной равнина
На юг,
На север памятив лесами.
Безмолвствуя певцом
(На вдохе задержав дыхание?),
Русалок наблюдать
На лунном берегу,
На солнечном — обыкновение мона́д.

                                        1997

A prairie spacious on the southern
Side,
Memorable for its woods to the north.
The silence of a singer
(Breathing held in a breath?)
To watch mermaids
On the lunar shore,
And on the solar one, an everyday monad.

1997

Краснеет и желтеет чернолéсье.
(Как некогда на одеяния —
И то сказать, изжита живость,
Но не ветреность —
За багрецом и золотом не постоял поэт.)
Сезон унылой
Зажиточности спорофитов
Встречать под пóлогом играющей листвы.

1997

The hardwoods turn yellow and red.
(As in the olden days on his attire —
So to speak, its liveliness toned down,
but not its giddiness —
the poet dispensed with crimson and gold.)
To meet the melancholy
Season when sporophytes prosper
Under a canopy of leaves at play.

1997

М. Ереминой

Течение вытачивает рыбу,
Вынашивает птицу ветер,
Земля
(Неповторимы дни Творения,
Поскольку вечны, си́речь закодировано
Во всякой тва́рной ма́трице
Несовершенство воспроизводимого.)
Свидетельствует абыолют зерна́.

1998

for M. Yeryomina

The current spins the fish,
The wind bears the bird,
The earth
(Not repeating the days of Creation,
Considering them as eternal, to wit
The imperfection of reproducing
Is encoded in every creaturely matrix)
Certifies the Absolute of the seed.

1998

Ириаде

Бывало, продолжался нежный сумрак пе́рголы
Сюжетом тканых выцветших обоев:
Пониже горнего, повыше дольнего
(В пределах заданных координат.),
На мотыльковых крылышках порхающие,
Упитанные купидоны́
(Закон Невтона оным не указ.)
Витают.

2001

for Iraida

The tender twilight of a pergola prolonged
sometimes by the subject of the faded fabric of shoes:
Lower than the hill, higher than the dale
(Co-ordinates within given limits)
On fluttering moth wings
Well fed little Cupids
(Not at the mercy of Newton's law)
Hover.

2001

Что до слепой стены (Окно —
Источник света
С восходом солнца для жильца,
В ночи — для гостя или пилигрима.),
То не исто́ргнутся и под ударами судьбы
Из не запроекти́рованного
(Ни створок, ни наличников.) проёма
Оско́льчатые слезы.

2002

What about the blind wall (The window
Is a source of light
At sunrise for the resident,
During the night — for a guest or a palmer.)
What are not expelled under the blows of fate
Through the absolutely unprepared
(neither panels nor casements) doorway
Are splintered tears.

2002

В. Герасимову

Рассказывают, что в развалинах
Дворцов и замков нечто или некто
Не существует, не живёт, но есть,
Мол, если нет, то соблаговолите
Дать объяснение тем голосам,
Которыми в урочные часы
Исходят
Фрагменты стен и сводов.

2004

for V. Gerasimov

They recount how in the ruins of palaces
And fortresses something or someone
Does not exist, does not live, but just is,
They say, if this is not so, then
Deign to explain the voices
That at certain hours
Sound within
These fragmented walls and vaults.

2004

Ириаде

Никак опять чару́ющ ландыш
В букете, бутонье́рке, вазе или склянке
Из-под Tincturæ Convallaria
(Период сбора от бутониза́ции
До эксплика́ции.) и в переле́сице,
Где неумо́лчного ручья, который
Окатывает экзерси́сный гравий краснословия,
Невнятна речь.

2004

for Iraida

The lily of the valley in no way again captivating
In a bouquet, boutonniere, vase or bottle
From under *Tincturæ Convallaria*
(A period of collection from budding
to explication.) and in a stand of trees,
Where in the uninterrupted brook
Practice pebbles of eloquence are flooded by
Indistinct speech.

2004

Ириаде

Потрескивал, искри́л (Избыток
Сели́тры или по́дмесь твёрдых углеводородов
Чрезмерна?)
В уюте сумерек фитиль, как вдруг электросве́т,
Который не древне́й ли, чем костры,
Лучины и лампады (Не во тьме ли довремён
Метали молнии предтечи громовержцев?),
Разоблачил свечу и выявил житейские углы.

2008

for Iraida

It crackled, it sparked (an excess
Of saltpetre or a grand sweep of hard
Hydrocarbons?)
A cozy wick of twilight, like sudden electriclight
No more ancient than campfires,
Kindling, and icon-lamps (Did the forerunners
Of metals fulminate not in the darkness of beforetime?)
Uncovered the candle and revealed ordinary corners.

2008

Ириаде

Когда предзи́мье гасит цвет за цветом,
Смири́ться с неизбежной убелённостью
Природы? Оболо́чь ли зябкие растения заботой
И защитить от выцветанья их наряды?
С дорукотво́рной дерзко потягаться
Поде́лочною красотою (Ква́рцевый песок,
Пота́ш и окислы тяжёлых
Металлов.), орешёченной свинцом?

2009

for Iraida

When will early winter extinguish color after color,
Submit to the inescapable grayness
Of nature? Will a shell shelter plants sensitive to cold
And protect against the fading of their attire?
Can the artificial be rivaled with impunity
By natural beauty (Quartz sand,
Potassium and oxides of heavy
Metals) laced with lead?

2009

Что делать с воробьи́ной стаей в кронах
Ручно́й работы? Сто́рожа с трещоткой подрядить?
Установить ли репродуктор с криком
Подра́нка об опастности? А что как птичий
Налёт есть проявленье благосклонности природы,
Что и сама на выдумки хитра, к трудам
(Ажу́рен силует, искусно вырезанный
Сека́тором. Затейливо изгонут штамб.) садовника?

2009

What to do with a flock of sparrows in hand-made
Treetops? Set a watchman with a rattle?
Or install a loudspeaker with the cry
Of one wounded in distress? And that like a bird's
Swoop is a manifestation of nature's favor,
That itself is a cunning invention, for the work
(A lacy silhouette, artfully cut out
By pruning shears. Intricately expel the trunk.) of the
    gardener?

2009

Окатанный допосейдоновым прибоем
Обломок огневого туфа (Горные горнила
Бесхозны в те поры́. Гефест не хром.),
Лукаво запелёнутый в лоскут (Сообщницей
Наречь ли безымянную ткачиху?),
Оторванный от старого оцовского хитона..., словом,
Издавние семейственные узы,
А то ещё рептилия живого яда вместо рыбы.

2009

Spewed out by the imposeidoned tide
The debris of fiery tufa (Mountain furnaces
Ownerless in those days. Hephaestus was not lame.),
Cunningly bubbled up in fragments (Name
As an accomplice an anonymous weaving woman?),
Cut off from the old ancestral chiton..., with a word,
Primordial family ties, but something more
A reptile of live venom instead of a fish.

2009

Приглядное созданье с терракотовою спинкой
И каолиновым брюшком,
Искусно, через ломкую соломнику,
Смакуя послевкусье, лакомится
Сгущенным солнцем, скопленным
По струйке злаком, или, воля ваша,
Прожорливая рыжая полёвка жадно
Терзает, то сторожко замирая, плоть растения.

2009

A creature revealed with a terracotta back
And a kaolin little belly,
Skillfully, through a brittle straw,
Enjoying the aftertaste, feasts
On concentrated sun, accumulated
In a trickle of cereal, or, if you please,
A voracious red vole
Ravages, watchfully, the flesh of the plant.

2009

Увидеть Lilium из трибы Lilieae
Как лилию в нетканом, из нерукотворных
Досоломоновых сокроищниц, наряде
И обрестись (Сколь дерзостно, столь мнимо.)
В единстве сущего
Промеж толиких и толик:
Иллузий и веществ, событий и галактик — в том,
Что есть не-эта-лилия.

2009

Consider *Lilium* of the tribe *Liliex*
As a lily in an unwoven array from
Unmanufactured pre-Solomonic treasuries,
And discover yourself (Bold, imaginary.)
In the unity of existence
Between the little and little enough:
Of illusions and substances, events and galaxies — In that
Which is not-this-lily.

2009

Прину́дить придорожный куст укутаться
Взаме́н листвы в зелёную с осенним
Оттенком шаль (Преображение подобно
Перемещению из воздуха в эфир.) и побудить
Не шелестеть, а пронимать проникновенным шепотом,
Нарушив безмятежное произрастание,
Назвать отцветшим или
Плодоносящим.

2009

Compel a roadside bush to be wrapped
Instead of in foliage in a green shawl
With a shade of autumn (Transfiguration is like
A transfer from air to ether.) And induce
Not to rustle, but with a piercing whisper penetrate
The broken undisturbed growth,
Call it faded or
Bearing fruit.

2009

Арéс ли некогда подбил на брань сестру, Эрѝда ли,
При попустительстве отца, в раздор втянула брата;
Мадам ли Mort, бывало, званым был герр Tod
На угощенье, тот ли по-соседски приглашал
Её на пиршество, — но ѝсстари доныне
(Порождена ли углерóдистым железом или
Органогенна нефт.) обыкновенны сводки
О павших.

2009

Whether Ares once incited his sister Eris to battle or
With the connivance of their father she pulled her brother
    into discord;
Whether Madame la Mort was bidden by Herr Tod
For a bite to eat, or he invited her as a neighbor
To a feast — but from time immemorial until now
(Whether generated by iron carbide or
biological oil.) lists of the fallen
Are commonplace.

                                                    2009

И будут, сказано, овéн и волк,
И лев, и вол питаться травной зéленью
И под оливами, которые
Перемогли, не хоронясь, потоп, бок о бок
Пережидать жару,
Но не ведёт ли равенство и братство
К нехватке жертв
И, стало быть, и к возвращенью страха?

2010

Ис. 11: 6–7
Быт. 1:30
Быт. 8:11

It is said, the wolf shall dwell with the lamb
And the lion shall eat green herb like the ox
Under olive trees that
Survived the Deluge, side by side
To wait out the heat,
But will not equality and fraternity lead
To a lack of sacrifice
And, consequently, to a return of fear?

2010

Isaiah 11: 6–7
Genesis 1:30
Genesis 8:11

Кому как не Афине было знать, что скрыто в голове
Отца? — Не у неё ли некто родом из Коло́на выведал,
Что про́мысел есть предсказание, а не предвидение?
Возможно, толки про утраченные знания
Не так уж праздны, даже если, скажем, и моро́чила
Уже не белопенная, ещё не беломраморная Афродита
В неё влюблённых смертных ро́ссказнями о придо́нных
Руинах.

                                                    2011

Who if not Athena was given to know what was hidden in the
    Father's
Head — Did someone born in Colonus worm out of her,
That providence is the craft is foretelling, not foresight?
Perhaps, gossip about lost meanings
Is so not idle, even if, let's say, Aphrodite,
No longer white-foamed but not white-stone, sowed confusion
In her mortal beloved folktales of the seabed's
Ruins.

2011

Что ви́дится прекрасным? Звёздный свод?
(Кому-то два пи эр квадрат,
Кому-то огранённый
Алмаз, в графе́новой, невесть зачем, обёртке.)
Что зна́ется за безобразное? Недо́лжное воочию?
(Бывает даже кошка некрасивой.) Стало быть,
Совме́стник совершенного
Подчас удачлив.

2012

What looks beautiful? A firmament of stars?
(To someone πr^2,
To someone else a well-cut
Diamond, who knows why, in a graphene setting.)
What's taken as disgusting? In the eye of the beholder? (Even
cats can pass for ugly.) And so,
the rival of the perfect
now and then succeeds.

2012

из какого сора — Ахматова

Пошедшие по штукатурке трещины
Наводят память то на кракелю́ры
(Иных времён от Бога мастера.),
То на погласшее, быв истолковано,
Насте́нное предначертание,
Тогда как вороватый
Прораб переборщил, видать, с уриной,
Да известь не была достаточно гашёной.

2012

... from what rubbish
Anna Akhmatova

Cracks all through the plasterwork
Suggest a memory sometimes of craquelure
(By God the master craftsman of other times.)
Sometimes of pronouncements, interpreted,
Destiny written on the wall,
When a thievish
Foreman went too far, see, using urine,
Even slaked lime would not do.

2012

Скрещенье цветоносных
Побегов кроны (Olea, Cassia, Boswellia etc).
Сплетенье брачных змей (И яблоко, тебе,
И капсулы целительного яда.).
Перинатальный самопряд и ралли шёлкового
Пути. Причудлив и пречу́ден —
Мироточенье —
Им данный мир.

2012

A criss-cross of flowerbearing
Crowning shoots (*Olea, Cassia, Boswellia* etc).
An interlacing of conjugal snakes (An apple, for you,
And capsules of medicinal poison).
Perinatal self-spinning and a rally on the silk
Road. Wound together and wondrous —
— Streaming myrrh —
His given world.

2012

Не потому ли не остановить мгновения,
Сколь ни было бы оное прекрасно,
Что время как побочный
Продукт при сотворенье мира
Сопутствует луны и солнца — (сутки, месяц, год.)
Но что греха таить, куда как соблазнительней
Гипо́тезы и до́мысли, и грёзы
О реверси́вном времени.

2012

Is it because there is no stopping moments
No matter how splendid this might be,
That time is like a by-
Product of the creation of the world,
Going along with the moon and the sun — days,
    months, years.
But we have to admit, how much more seductive
Hypotheses and conjectures, even dreams
About reversing time.

2012

Вода, блуждая в небе, отражается
Везде в себе самое, и в биотеле,
И в луже на просевшем
или Тихом океане. Не за то ли
Мирское время дрéвле добывали
За каплей капля из дырявого сосуда
Как частное — вода,
Делённая на скорость истечения?

2012

Water, wandering through the sky, gets reflected
Everywhere in itself, in a living body
Or in a puddle on uneven
Pavement or in the Pacific ocean. Isn't that why
The ancients determined worldly time
Drop by drop from a leaking vessel
As something particular — water,
Divided by the rate of flow?

2012

Лиса экстраполи́рует, где перехватит зайца.
Голодные щенки её удачу предвкушают. Крыси
Спасаются, предчувствуя неладное. Предсмотрительности
Обязаны наличием замки́ и за́мки. Предрекают
Пророки руини́рованье артефактов.
Что есть предвидение? —
Житейская ли прозорливость?
Приоткрове́ние ли Про́мысла, попу́щенное смертным?

2012

The fox anticipates where to intercept the hare.
Her hungry pups look forward to her luck. Rats
Save themselves, sensing something wrong. Prognostications
Are owed to the presence of locks and castles. Prophets
Foretell the destruction of artifacts.
What is prediction? —
Is it everyday perspicacity?
A glimpse of Providence, permitted to mortals?

2012

Действительные обитатели мостов —
Зеваки и самоубийцы. Рыболовов
Не жалуют блюстители порядка. Прочий люд —
Переезжает или переходит, ибо всякий мост,
Что перекинут через реку ли, дорогу ли,
По сути, есть отрезок,
Случается, последний в жизни,
Проложенного к пункту Б из пункта А, пути.

2013

The real inhabitants of bridges
Are sightseers and suicides. Fishermen
Are not in favor with the guardians of order. Other folk —
Move on or move over, for every bridge
That spans a river, or spans a road,
In fact, is a segment,
It happens, late in life,
Laid down to point B from point A, on the journey.

2013

Ираиде

Поскольку был великий сфинкс задуман неподвластным
Тысячелетьям (К слову, известняк не лучший выбор.),
Во исполненье дерзостного замысла предосудительно ли
Утраты возвращать, дото́шно сколы (Тест
На расовую совестимость носа.) восполнять, не дорожа́
Вмешательством песчаных бурь, потопов,
      злоумышленников?
А что до Сфи́нги, то её останками
Пусть озабочиваются патологоанатомы.

2013

for Iraida

As long as the great sphinx was conceived to be not subject
To millennia (Incidentally, limestone not the best choice.)
In carrying out an impudent scheme is it reprehensible
To return what was lost, meticulously chipped (Test
The racial shamefulness of the nose.) to fill in without
    respecting
The intervention of sandstorms, floods, mischiefmakers?
As far as Sphinga goes, let those remains
Trouble the anatomical pathologists.

2013

Негаданная встреча с привидением (Глухое
Безлюдье. Полночь. Молнии.) кого ни ошарашит —
Вестимо, бродят неприкаянными душегу́бцы
Отьявленные, жертвы не отмщённые, скупцы,
Что и по смерти стерегут секретные сокровища,
Под пару коим тени неуёмных
Кладоискательей, тогда как считано
Являемы верги́лии.

2014

An unexpected meeting with a ghost (Dismal
Wilderness. Midnight. Lightning.) will flabbergast anyone —
Of course, miraculously appearing hitmen,
Unavenged victims, and misers roam around,
Keeping their secret treasures even in death,
Under a vapor in which the shadows of irrepressible
Treasure hunters, who might be appearing
As Vergilian guides.

2014

Растения привержены геоцентри́зму,
Взять, скажем, яблоню — от ве́ка,
Будь то в эде́мских насаждениях,
И во владеньях Геспери́д,
В предгорьях Алата́у,
В садах ли графства Ли́нкольншир,
Проростком направляем корень,
По Птолеме́ю, к центру мироздания.

2015

Plants are committed to geocentrism,
Take, say, an apple tree — down through the ages,
Whether planted in Eden,
In the realm of the Hesperides,
In the foothills of the Alatau ranges,
In the orchards of County Lincolnshire,
We orient the root as a seedling,
Following Ptolemy, to the center of the universe.

2015

Nomina si nescis periit et cognitio rerum.
Carolus Linnaeus

Соцветия голо́вчатые; сте́бель
Прямостоячий, полый; листья
Трехлопастные, опушённые с испо́да —
Пастух и пахарь, вол и шмель
Определяли вкус и запах, цвет и форму,
Дабы одна из тва́рных трав
Означала была бы (Trifolium pratense)
Как сущая.

2015

Nomina si nescis periit et cognitio rerum.
Carolus Linnaeus

The inflorescences are capitate; the stem
Erect, hollow; leaves
Three-lobed, powdery underneath —
Shepherd and plowman, ox and bumblebee
Distinguished the taste and smell, the color and shape
So that one of the created herbs
Might be taken *(Trifolium pratense)*
As genuine.

2015

... ноябрь уж у двора
А. С. Пушкин

На лёд — ни лапой вольный гусь, предпочитая
Скользить по лону южных вод.
От рощи — ки́новарь по золоту —
Осталась про́рись —
Весне наказанный кано́н,
Но Мастер возрождения
Нарушит кроны свежими побегами
Под пра́зелень.

2015

...November is already in the dooryard
A. S. Pushkin

Onto the ice — not the foot-free goose, preferring
To glide on the bosom of southern waters.
From the grove — cinnabar on gold —
A tracing still remained —
the canon prescribed for spring,
But the Master of rebirth
Breaks through the crowns with fresh shoots
Dappled green.

2015

Сакральные курти́ны, рощи и дубравы
В долгу у ревностных аде́птов
За и́стовое почитание
И в страхе, что за промедленье в исполненье мольб,
Того гляди, сведут под корень
Нетерпеливые поклонники. Товарный древосто́й
Зависит от лесопромышленников.
Но где-то, говорят, живётся во́льно самосе́ву.

2016

ЛК РФ, 2:15; 1.16,19

Sacred plantings, groves and stands of oak
In the service of zealous experts
For deep veneration
And in fear of delay in the fulfillment of their prayers,
Go and look, impatient devotees will take down
To the root. Merchandising old growth
Depends on timber merchants.
But somewhere, they say, freely self-seeding.

2016

Forestry Regulations of the Russian Federation, 2:15; 1.16.19

Общи́ны малых горожан, таких как, скажем, голуби и
      крысы,
Довольствуются по́едью с людского, но и подворовывая,
Стола. Не приживутся ни заблудший лось, ни ше́ршень,
Попавший в западню трамвайного вагона, ибо первый росл
И яр, второй и нелюдим, и жа́лист. Что ни щель в асфальте,
Не медля, пробивные терния из местных
Укореняются. Горчичное зерно, залётное
Ни весть откуда, не проклюнулось.

2016

Communities of small city-dwellers, such as, let's say, pigeons
    and rats,
Satisfy their need for food, but by thieving, from the human
Table. A disoriented elk will not adapt, nor a hornet
Trapped in a westbound streetcar, for the first is hulky
And furious, the second unsociable and stinging. Wherever
there's a gap in the asphalt
Penetrating indigenous weeds take root
Right away. Mustard seed wafted in
From who knows where did not hatch out.

2016

Когда колючие кусты не заколдо́ванно,
А сами по себе
Цепляются к ночному путнику
И тот сбивается с тропы́,
И оморо́ченный, кружа́, клянет
То излучение загадочных антени,
То нечто внеземное, не обидно ли
За нечисть де́брей и болот, и о́мутов?

2017

When thorn bushes are not bewitched,
But on their own
Catch at the nocturnal traveler
Until he misses the pathway
And is confounded, circling, and swears
It's either radiation from mysterious antennæ
Or something unearthly, doesn't it offend
The evil spirit of thickets, swamps, and eddies?

2017

И всяко было слово — и наска́льным, и резьбой
По кости, и на писчей глине выдавленным,
И на папи́русе, пергаменте, бумаге, и берёсте
Начертанным, и закоди́рованным
(Тире и точке, флажный семафор и прочее),
И оцифро́ванным. И было слово
Явле́нное и, быв раско́лото в сердца́х,
По памяти воспроизведено́.

2017

Исх. 32:19

And each word was — on rock, and in carvings
On bone, and on extruded clay tablets,
And on papyrus, parchment, paper, and birchbark
Inscribed and coded
(Dash and dot, flag semaphore, and so on),
And digitized. And the word was
Made manifest and, having been riven in their hearts,
Recreated from memory.

2017

Exodus 32:19

Неколебимо, как Россия.
А. С. Пушкин

И дельта вроде как не дельта
(Со сведущими спорить толку нет),
И под гранитной, мраморной, кирпичной кладкой,
И под брусчатым, и асфальтым застилом,
По сути, топь, и хлябь. Чему обязан град,
Твердостоя́ньем (сгон, нагон ли вод ли, зол)?
Расчёту корабелов? Риску зодчих?
Что было ве́домо поэту?

2017

Unshakable, like Russia.
A. S. Pushkin

And the delta is not like a delta
(No sense arguing with experts)
And under granite, marble, brickwork,
And under cobblestones, and asphalt paving,
In essence, it's marsh, and swamp. To what does the city owe
Its endurance (ebb and flow of either waters or ash)?
The calculation of shipbuilders? The gamble of architects?
What did the poet know?

                                                    2017

Памяти Торопова Н. М.

Шевеля кандалами цеповек дверных...
Осип Мандельштам

Не трубный глас, а хрипловатое вещание
Домашних репродукторов. Землетрясений ни за балл
Сейсмографы не зафиксировали. Острова́
Не дрейфова́ли. Молнии и гро́мы исходили
По мѐтеопричи́нам. Туча саранчо́вая не накрывала го́рода.
И ни один из бронзовых коней не напугал
Кого-то львиной пастью в те года́ не столь угрозных
    улиц,
Сколь жуткой беззащитости жилищ.

2017

Откр. 6, 7, 8, 9

In memory of N. M. Toropov

Rattling the shackles of door chains...
Osip Mandelstam

Not the voice of a trumpet, but a squawking broadcast
On home sound systems. Earthquakes did not
Register on seismographs. Islands
Did not drift. Lightning and thunder accorded with
Weather conditions. Swarms of locusts did not cover the city.
And not one of the bronze steeds terrified
With lion's teeth during years not so much of dangerous
    streets,
As of a dreadful defenselessness of dwellings.

2017

Rev. 6, 7, 8, 9

Дела давно минувших дней...
А. С. Пушкин

У прохивавших на Олимпе, скажем, дам
Божественных, но не чура́вшихся
Земных соблазнов, не была ли ветреная муза
Верба́льной страстности и соблазняющих гримас
В любимицах? Трагикомические маски,
Скорей, по нраву площадному люду. Реквизит —
Раз навсегда. Репертуар —
Едва не наизусть от альфы до омеги.

2017

Matters of days long gone by...
A. S. Pushkin

Among those divine ladies who dwelled on Olympus,
let's say, but not steering clear
Of earthly temptations, whether there was a windy muse
Of verbal passion and favorite seductive
Grimaces? Tragicomic masks,
Rather, to the liking of vulgar people. The props —
Once and for all. The repertoire —
Almost by rote from alpha to omega.

2017

Неве́сть зачем, ещё поддерживают стены
Не живописный некогда плафон,
А серый потолок в разводах от протечек,
Осыпался витражный о́кулюс (парили чайки
На ясном небосводе, коего осколки
Вдруг и сверкнут в грязи и лужах по́ла),
Сквозь переплёт дыры́ — то свет луны́, то звёзды,
То грозовые тучи, но в солнечное небо.

2017

Who knows why, the walls still support
Not a quondam picturesque decorated *plafond,*
But a gray ceiling falling apart from leaks,
The stained glass oculus showered (seagulls soared
In a clear sky, fragments of which
Suddenly sparkle in the mud and puddles on the floor),
Through the frame of the hole — moonlight, starlight,
Or thunderclouds, but in a sunny sky.

2017

Всё нет покою одиноко перестойному над пóлогом
(Сомкнулись кроны жердняка́.) — то малый зверь балу́ет
В листве, то нáбольший когти́т кору́, то чей-то клюв
Выстукивает пропитание, и в бóрти до заката
Несносная возня. А как зати́шье (от ночных
До предрассветных травей), та́ки
Как не прислушиваться к старческому хру́сту
Своих ветвей?

2017

All is not calm for the lone tree overtopping the canopy
(The crowns of stem exclusion closed in) — here a small animal
Chatters in the foliage, there a larger one claws the bark, a beak
Clatters for food, and a hollow in the trunk during daylight
Is unbearably busy. But in a short silence (from nocturnal
To predawn grasses) how
Not to pay attention to the decrepit crackling
Of its branches?

2017

TABLE OF CONTENTS

Mikhail Fyodorovich Yeryomin [Михаил Фёдорович Ерёмин] was born in 1936 in the northern Caucasus but grew up in Leningrad, where he graduated from the Herzen Institute. The first volume of his poems (in Russian) was published in the United States in 1986, and then in 1991 in Moscow. Each book is a cumulative edition to and a selection from his previous work, and each carries the same title: *Stikhotvorenia (Poems)*.

Yeryomin, who has been awarded both the Andrey Bely Prize and a Joseph Brodsky Memorial Fellowship, lives in St. Petersburg.

J. Kates is a poet, a literary translator and the co-director of Zephyr Press. He has been awarded three National Endowment for the Arts Fellowships, an Individual Artist Fellowship from the New Hampshire State Council on the Arts, and the Cliff Becker Book Prize in Translation. He has published three chapbooks of his own poems and one full book, *The Briar Patch* (Hobblebush Books). He is the translator of a dozen books of translations of Russian and French poets, and has edited two anthologies of translations. He has also collaborated on four books of Latin American poetry in translation.

BLACK WIDOW PRESS :: MODERN POETRY SERIES

WILLIS BARNSTONE
ABC of Translation
African Bestiary (forthcoming)

DAVE BRINKS
The Caveat Onus
The Secret Brain: Selected Poems 1995–2012

RUXANDRA CESEREANU
Crusader-Woman. Translated by Adam J.
  Sorkin. Introduction by Andrei Codrescu.
Forgiven Submarine by Ruxandra Cesereanu
  and Andrei Codrescu.

CLAYTON ESHLEMAN
An Alchemist with One Eye on Fire
Anticline
Archaic Design
Clayton Eshleman/The Essential Poetry:
  1960–2015
Grindstone of Rapport: A Clayton Eshleman
  Reader
Penetralia
Pollen Aria
The Price of Experience
Endure: Poems by Bei Dao. Translated by
  Clayton Eshleman and Lucas Klein.
Curdled Skulls: Poems of Bernard Bador.
  Translated by Bernard Bador with
  Clayton Eshleman.

PIERRE JORIS
Barzakh (Poems 2000–2012)
Exile Is My Trade: A Habib Tengour Reader

MARILYN KALLET
Even When We Sleep (forthcoming)
How Our Bodies Learned
Packing Light: New and Selected Poems
The Love That Moves Me
Disenchanted City (La ville désenchantée)
  by Chantal Bizzini. Translated by
  J. Bradford Anderson, Darren Jackson,
  and Marilyn Kallet.

ROBERT KELLY
Fire Exit
The Hexagon

STEPHEN KESSLER
Garage Elegies
Last Call

BILL LAVENDER
Memory Wing

HELLER LEVINSON
from stone this running
LinguaQuake
Lure (forthcoming)
Lurk
jus' sayn' (forthcoming)
Seep
Tenebraed
Un-
Wrack Lariat

JOHN OLSON
Backscatter: New and Selected Poems
Dada Budapest
Larynx Galaxy
Weave of the Dream King

NIYI OSUNDARE
City Without People: The Katrina Poems
Green: Sighs of Our Ailing Planet: Poems

MEBANE ROBERTSON
An American Unconscious
Signal from Draco: New and Selected Poems

JEROME ROTHENBERG
Concealments and Caprichos
Eye of Witness: A Jerome Rothenberg Reader.
  Edited with commentaries by Heriberto
  Yepez & Jerome Rothenberg.
The President of Desolation & Other Poems

AMINA SAÏD.
The Present Tense of the World: Poems 2000–2009.
Translated with an introduction by
Marilyn Hacker.

ANIS SHIVANI
Soraya (Sonnets)

JERRY W. WARD, JR.
Fractal Song

BLACK WIDOW PRESS :: ANTHOLOGIES / BIOGRAPHIES

*Barbaric Vast & Wild: A Gathering of Outside and
Subterranean Poetry (Poems for the Millennium,* vol. 5).
Jerome Rothenberg and John Bloomberg-Rissman,
editors.

Clayton Eshleman: The Whole Art by Stuart Kendall

Revolution of the Mind: The Life of André Breton
by Mark Polizzotti